Bake Sale

Contents

Mallow snowmen

Ingredients

White marshmallows (A 106g bag makes 6-7 snowmen)

Cake decorations for eyes and buttons etc
(I cut little slices off a toffee bar for the arms on the taller snowmen, or I have used pieces of liquorice which also works well. Or you could cut up some Matchmakers or chocolate mint/orange sticks.)

Small-sized digestive biscuits or other type of plain biscuit
(NOTE: if you use gluten-free biscuits, label them as such and strictly separate them from snowmen that are on ordinary biscuits. Keep the original packet under the table to show customers if they query it.)

Sweet cases to use as hats. Marzipan carrots, chocolate drops or anything else you wish to use as decoration.

Recipe

1. Melt several marshmallows in a heatproof bowl over a simmering pan of water or melt in a microwave. This will be used as the 'glue' to stick everything together. Only do small batches at a time because it cools quickly and you will find it difficult to work with.

2. Because working with the melted mallow can be messy, it is best to decorate the 'faces' and 'bodies' first.

3. For the 'melted snowmen' spread a generous amount of the melted mallow over the biscuit, press on the decorated faces (they should be unhappy faces!) and decorate the melted mallow with a small marzipan carrot or some chocolate chips, to show that his nose and buttons have melted off his body.

4. For the 'unmelted' snowmen, you will need to decorate three mallows first – the face and two 'bodies', with 'buttons', 'eyes' etc.

5. On one of the bodies you need to put a small blob of melted mallow on either side and gently press in whatever you are using to make arms.

6. Spread some melted mallow over the biscuit base (but less than for the 'melted snowmen'.)

7. Add the first 'body' mallow to the base, put a large blob of melted mallow on top of it and gently press on the second 'body' mallow.

8. Put a large blob on top of the second 'body' mallow and gently press on the 'head' mallow.

9. Leave all the constructed snowmen to firm up before you add large blobs of melted mallow and put the sweet cases in place as hats – making sure the 'melted snowmen look as though their hats are slipping off!

10. Add whatever extra decoration you wish. The scarves, although not edible in this picture, could be if you used strips of fruit leathers.

No—Bake Chocolate Peanut Butter Cake

Have you had those small chocolate peanut butter filled discs?
Very sweet, very moreish! Well, this is a huge one of them!!!
(Or you could split the mixture up and make lots of individual cakes).

Ingredients

1lb 2ozs (500g) icing sugar

5ozs (140g) salted butter

21ozs (600g) peanut butter

23ozs (650g) milk chocolate

Recipe

1. You need a 9 inch (23 cms) flan tin with a removable base (if you are doing the large cake, which you will cut into slices to sell). Line the base of tin with baking parchment and grease sides well.

2. Mix the sugar, peanut butter and butter together and it will form a stiff dough.

3. Melt three-quarters of the chocolate in a Pyrex, enamel or steel bowl, over a pan of hot water.

4. When melted, pour the chocolate into the flan tin and smooth to cover base.

5. When it has slightly cooled and is no longer liquid, gently push some of the chocolate up the edge of the tin with a spoon, making sure that you don't create any holes in the base. Place the tin lined with chocolate into the fridge for at least 20mins, to set.

6. Once you are sure that it is set, <u>carefully</u> remove the chocolate shell from the tin and set aside.

7. Press the peanut dough into the empty flan tin, until it is flat and is touching the sides of tin.

8. Then, with a sharp knife, cut away approximately a quarter of an inch (Approximately 6 mm) all way around the edge, so that you have a gap between the dough and the sides of the tin.

9. Carefully place the disc of peanut dough into the chocolate case making sure there's a gap around edge and the peanut dough is not higher than the sides of the chocolate case.

10. Wipe flan tin clean and place the whole chocolate peanut cake (chocolate case included) carefully back in the flan tin.

11. Melt the remaining chocolate in a bowl over hot water (see No.3 above) and pour over the top of the peanut dough filling, trying to not pour it over the chocolate casing but, at the same time, making sure the peanut dough is completely covered.

12. Smooth with pallet knife and decorate with anything you want before returning it to the fridge to set. and return to fridge to set.

13. When slicing the cake into individual portions, try and warm the knife first, to avoid the chocolate from cracking. If you have no facility to do that on your stall, then it might be best to cut the cake up and wrap the portions before leaving home, or make the individual versions of this recipe. (If you use the small foil cupcake cases, you can coat each of them with melted chocolate and then follow the instructions for the large cake recipe).

Nut Brittle
(stove top only)

This is always a favourite. So easy to make and sell! But, be very careful of hot toffee splashes that can burn the skin of your hands and forearms. We recommend that you use a long handled wooden spoon and don't have the heat too high so that you just get a gentle boiling and bubbling of the mixture. If you want to you could wear long oven gloves for the boiling part of the recipe.

Ingredients

2½ozs (70g) butter
6½ozs (180g) caster sugar
7ozs (200g) Golden Syrup
7oz (200g) peanuts (best to use unsalted if you can – or you can use any nuts or mixture of nuts)
1 tablespoon (15ml) water.

Recipe

1. Melt butter and sugar over a gentle heat. (Use a long handled wooden spoon)

2. Add the syrup when butter and sugar have mixed well and are slightly bubbling.

3. Stir thoroughly and bring gently to the boil.

4. When you have a rolling boil (continuous bubbles), drop a tiny portion of the mixture off the tip of spoon into a glass of iced (very cold) water. If the mixture forms into a hard ball, then it is time to stir in the peanuts. If you can squeeze the ball into another shape, like fudge, then boil the mixture a little more and repeat the test in a few minutes.

5. Move the pan off of the hot hob on to a cold one whilst you stir the peanuts in. Make sure they are all coated well, then put the pan back on the hot hob to boil a little, as adding the nuts whilst off the hob will have taken the temperature down a little.

6. Then do the drop test into the iced water again with the now nutty mix.

7. If successful (goes to hard ball) pour into a greased baking tray lined with baking parchment.

8. Leave to set for up to an hour.

9. Ready for the best bit? Get cracking! Smash and grab.

10. Weigh the broken pieces into equal portions and bag them in cellophane bags, or select the same number of equal-sized portions and bag them up.

Cheese straws
(cheats version)

Making puff pastry from scratch is such a labour of love. If you like doing it, then fine, but we are recommending ready-made puff pastry if you have lots to make for a Bake Sale and not much time. We also recommend that you make largish cheese straws. If you make them too thin they will break up into crumbs before you can get them to the sale!

Ingredients

Pack (or packs) of defrosted frozen puff pastry.

Half a teaspoon of salt

Large pinch of pepper

A large pinch of Cayenne pepper/or English mustard powder (your preference and could be optional but either does complement the flavor of the cheese)

4½ozs (125gms) strong cheddar cheese (per pack of puff pastry)

A beaten egg

Recipe

1. Pre-heat oven to 230C (450F Gas Mark 8).

2. Roll out pastry into a large rectangle.

3. In a bowl, grate the cheese and sprinkle your chosen condiment over it. Stir it a bit to make sure the cheese and pepper/mustard is fully blended.

4. Sprinkle the rectangle of pastry with half of the cheese mix, then fold the rectangle over twice (top to bottom) and roll it out again into a large rectangle.

5. Sprinkle remaining cheese mix on the top and press it lightly into the surface.

6. Cut the rectangle into ¾inch (2cms) wide strips, gently lift on to a baking tray lined with parchment, leaving space between each one.

7. Lightly brush with beaten egg.

8. Pop in oven for approximately 15 minutes. (Keep eye on them though because the cheese can burn very quickly.)

9. When cool, either tie them up in batches, or bag three or four in cellophane to display and sell..Scrumptious!

Cat treats

You would amazed at how many people jump at the chance to buy treats for their pets at bake sales! This treat for your cat is very, very easy.

Ingredients

1 x 5.5 - 6ozs (155 - 170g) tin of tuna, drained
8ozs (225g) wholemeal flour
1 egg
2-3 tablespoons of water
1 heaped tablespoon of cat nip
Small cat mixer biscuits cut in half for the eyes.

Recipe

1   Mix all ingredients together in a bowl.

2   Then gently roll out the mixture on a floured work surface until it is about ¼ inch (5mm) thick.

3.   Then cut out your shapes. Any shapes you like – either with a cutter or by hand. Don't make them too large. Cats prefer something smallish, like the size of a medium button, or a small fish shape, but their owners will be attracted by biscuits that are cat shaped!

4.   Decorate, if required.

5.   Bake for approximately 15 minutes at 350F (180C Gas Mark 4).

6.   Allow to cool and bag up for selling.

Flapjacks

These always sell so well. Golden squares of sweetness that everybody loves! And so easy to make. This recipe makes approximately 24 squares.

Ingredients

8ozs (225g) butter
8ozs (225g) brown sugar
3ozs (85g) Golden Syrup
10ozs (300g) porridge oats

Recipe

1. Pre-heat the oven to 325F (170C or Gas Mark 3).

2. In a saucepan, over a low heat, melt butter and sugar together.

3. Then add syrup and stir until everything is nicely combined.

4. Then stir in the porridge oats.

5. Scrape into a greased 12 x 9inch (30cms x 23cms) baking/roasting tin.

6. Bake for 35 mins making sure they do not overbake (get too brown and dry)

7. When slightly warm, cut into squares.

8. Pop each square in a bag, tie with a ribbon or seal with a festive sticker.

Hokey Pokey or Cinder Toffee (stove top)

My Mother used to sing the Hokey Pokey Song to us, and all the small children that touched her life. It was a knee bouncer!

Hokey Pokey Penny a Lump
That's the stuff to make you jump.
If you jump you're bound to fall
Hokey Pokey says it all.

Those little shards of golden cinder toffee that dissolve in your mouth are so yummy. Try crumbling it over ice cream! So quick and easy to make.

Ingredients

3ozs (85g) caster sugar
1ozs (30g) soft light brown sugar
4 tablespoons of Golden Syrup
1½ teaspoons of bicarbonate of soda
White chocolate for decoration
Edible lustre

Recipe

1. Put all ingredients in to a saucepan (except the bicarbonate of soda) and stir to mix together, before you turn on the heat.

2. Turn on heat fairly high and leave it to bubble away for a little while. It will turn golden and smooth with tiny bubbles popping on the surface. Let it bubble away until it is a rolling mass of big bubbles.

3. The mixture must be the right heat for it to set, so use a kitchen / toffee thermometer, place into the pan and watch.

4. As soon as the heat reaches 150C (300F) take the pan off the heat, quickly add the bicarb of soda and whisk until it puffs up to a lovely foamy mass.

5. Turn out the mixture quickly into a baking tray lined with baking parchment and let it set. It should be about 1inch (2cms) thick.

6. It will take approximately one hour to set.

7. Then the fun bit! Smashing it to bite size lumps!

8. Put into fancy bags or paper cones, to sell on your stall.

9. For Christmas bake sales, I melt white chocolate and dip or drizzle it over, or dip bigger pointed chunks in melted white chocolate mixed with a little squirt of edible lustre. Hey presto! Christmas Mountains at the North Pole. Enjoy.

Rich brown lemon curd

The colour of this lemon curd is caused by using rich dark brown sugar or molasses sugar. If you want traditional yellow lemon curd, then use white caster sugar. Personally, I discovered that using dark sugar gives the curd a lovely rich, sweet taste which contrasts with the sharpness of the lemons. Also, if used as a cake filler it looks like chocolate and gives the eater a lovely surprise when they taste lemon!
The recipe makes 4 small jars.

Ingredients

4 unwaxed lemons

4 eggs

12ozs (340g) rich dark brown or molasses sugar (see opposite for yellow curd)

12ozs (340g) unsalted butter

Half teaspoon of vanilla essence

Recipe

1. Cut the lemons, extract the juice and gently grate the skins to get the zest. (I like my zest a mix of thin and thick but it's entirely up to you.)

2. Beat the eggs in a cup.

3. Put all the ingredients – Lemon zest, juice, beaten eggs, sugar, butter and vanilla essence – in a heatproof bowl, over a large pan of simmering water. (Do not have the heat too high or you may inadvertently cook the eggs!)

4. Using a wooden spoon, stir gently, once the butter has melted, and continue to stir for about 20 minutes until the curd thickens up.

5. For Autumn and Christmas bake fairs, I add a clove to each jar and either add large pinch of cinnamon to the ingredients before cooking or push a small stick into each jar.

6. Cover the lid of the jars with fabric, waxed paper, or paint them gold. You could tie a cinnamon stick to the jar with a ribbon or make a tag the shape and colour of a lemon.

NOTE: It is advisable to create a label for jars of curd, jam or other preserves, detailing the exact ingredients in order to inform people who may have allergies. For example, a customer may not be aware that curds have egg in them and that could be a problem for some people, like vegans.

Dog Biscuits

Dogs deserve healthy treats, just like humans, so we recommend that you perhaps use gluten free flour and pet peanut butter (made especially for pets, with no added sugar or salt, and available through most large pet shops). Don't overfeed dogs any treats – even the healthy ones!

Ingredients

1lb(450g) of gluten free flour (preferably wholemeal, if you can get it)

1 teaspoon of baking powder

Approximately 1 standard teacup cup full of pet peanut butter.

A standard teacup of water

2 tablespoons of honey

1 large egg.

Recipe

1   Pre-heat oven to 325F (160C or Gas Mark 3)

2.   Mix all the ingredients together in large bowl until the mixture forms a soft dough.

3.   Roll out the dough, on a floured board, to approximately ½inch (1 cm) thick, and cut into shapes. This dough is firm and doesn't spread in the oven, so you can do some quite elaborate cookie designs.

4.   Place the cookies on a baking tray, lined with baking parchment, leaving some space between each.

5.   Bake for approximately 20 minutes. Don't allow them to get too brown. (Your dog won't mind but they sell better if they are a golden colour!)

I've used Pug and French bulldog designs, but the choice is yours. Store in airtight container for your own use at home. They sell so well because they make great little gifts for pampered pups! I usually package them in cellophane bags, tied with a bow and clearly marked as dog biscuits, with the ingredients listed.

Rock Cakes

There is nothing more perfect than a rock cake with a nice cup of tea. (Except perhaps a split and buttered rock cake with a cup of tea!) The humble rock cake is an old-fashioned teatime treat that often gets overlooked, nowadays, in favour of more exotic things but they are so quick and easy to make. This batch is fruit-free, as my daughter doesn't like dried fruits or spices, so I've added choc chips, candy coated chocolate counters, a few white chocolate buttons, and I've decorated them with chocolate balls or a handful of festive coloured balls. When I make traditional mixed-fruit, slightly spiced, rock cakes, the only decoration I add is a sprinkle of demerara sugar.

Ingredients

- 8ozs (225g) of plain flour
- ½ teaspoon of salt
- 2 teaspoons of baking powder
- 6ozs (170g) brown sugar
- 6ozs (170g) butter (straight from the fridge)
- 1 large egg
- 5oz (140g) mixed dried fruit (if making the fruit version), otherwise use a small pack of choc chips, a small pack of white chocolate buttons and a handful of candy covered chocolate counters.
- 1 teaspoon of mixed spice and a pinch of nutmeg (if making the fruit ones)
- 1-2 tablespoons of milk

Recipe

1. Preheat the oven to 325F (170C or Gas Mark 3)

2. Put the mixed fruit or the sweets to one side for the moment.

3. Beat the egg in a cup on its own.

4. Put the flour, salt, baking powder and cold, chopped-up butter in a mixing bowl and rub the mixture between your fingers until it resembles breadcrumbs.

5. Stir in the fruit, (or sweets) and the sugar, making sure that it is all blended.

6. Then stir in the milk and add the beaten egg.

7. Mix the mixture together with your hands, then take small handfuls and put them, spaced apart on to baking tray, lined with baking parchment.

8. Bake for around 18-20 minutes.

9. When cool, pack them in a tin lined with some fancy doilies and sell them individually.

Festive Mince Parcels

These are lovely and easy. Quick to make and gorgeous when eaten warm with a scoop of ice cream or brandy butter. Very popular at Bake Sales because some people don't like a lot of pastry on their mince pies.

Ingredients

1 Pack of Filo Pastry Sheets.
1 beaten egg
Icing sugar to dust
A jar of luxury mincemeat.

Recipe

1. Pre heat oven to 350F (180C or Gas Mark 4)

2. Open out the Filo sheets and cut into squares of about 4 inches (10 cms).

3. Take 4 of the squares, brush each one with a little beaten egg and lay on top of each other, each layer at an angle, so that they form a sort of star shape.

4. Spoon a heaped teaspoon of mincemeat in the centre of the filo squares.

5. Bring up the sides of the pastry and scrunch together, rather like a paper bag and twist slightly, to make sure that the layers stay together.

6. Brush the whole parcel with a little more beaten egg.

7. Repeat until you have used up all your filo pastry squares.

8. Place all the parcels on a baking tray lined with greaseproof paper, a little way apart from each other to allow the hot air to circulate.

9. Bake for approximately 20 minutes

10. Remove from oven and, when cool, dust with icing sugar.

11. Be careful when handling them as the crisp tops can be quite fragile and crumble easily. But you can add ribbon around the neck of the parcels if you wish.

12. We suggest that you sell them in little boxes or stiff paper bags, so that they make it home in one piece!

Funny Fondant Faces

No cooking required! (The greatest words you can hear when you have to get a batch of things ready for a bake stall!) These will fly off the table at a Bake Sale. Children love to pick the funny faces they want. Don't be surprised if you get orders for children's parties afterwards.

Ingredients

Biscuits, (plain digestive biscuits are a good idea)

A pack of fondant ready-to-roll icing. (White is a good because you can add colour when you need it)

A large pack of marshmallows

Some fruit jam (to 'glue' fondant to biscuit)

Icing pens or piping bag with fine nozzle.

A few sweets and edible decorations.

Paper cake cases to use as hats/collars/fans.

Recipe

1. Divide the icing into small balls if you wish to add colour to some of it.

2. Using a cocktail stick slowly dip and add colour to the white icing a little at a time until desired colour is reached.

3. Roll the icing balls out to the size of biscuit. Spread a smear of jam all over the top of the biscuit and add the fondant circle.

4. Now, let your artistic side take over and make clowns, farm animals, funny faces, aliens, monsters, flowers etc. We have the examples in the picture and a few ideas below. (The frog face in the photo was sprayed with a little edible lustre to give him a reptilian sheen. Ears, hats and other protrusions, need to be tucked between the biscuit and the icing.)

Ideas below from www.firstpalette.com

Cheese and Rosemary Scones

These are lush and very popular as a lunchtime snack-on-the-go at a Bake Sale! The parmesan is optional, but it does give an extra cheesy tang. It's best sprinkled over the scones when they come straight from the oven, so that the heat makes the parmesan melt slightly into the tops of the scones. When making any kind of scones, use cold butter and do not over-knead the dough. If offering them as a portable lunch snack, or afternoon tea, consider offering them split and buttered with a small piece of extra cheese and some chutney or pickles.

Ingredients

13ozs (370g) plain or wholemeal flour
1tsp baking powder
Half tsp mild paprika
Good pinch of salt
2ozs (55g) cold butter (cubed)
1 beaten egg
Three quarters of a standard teacup of grated cheddar.
½ pint (250ml) room temperature milk
1-2 tablespoons of fresh fine chopped rosemary.
Grated parmesan.

Recipe

1   Pre heat oven to 200C (400F or Gas Mark 6) and line baking trays with greaseproof/ baking parchment.

2   Put all the dry ingredients (except the parmesan) into a bowl.

3   Rub in the cold cubes of butter until the mixture resembles breadcrumbs.

4   Add the beaten egg and half of the milk and stir, bringing the mixture together to form a firm dough.

5   Shape the dough (lightly knead into a ball), turn out in floured surface and roll out to approximately 1 inch thick (2.5cms) thick and cut into shapes.

6   Transfer to the baking trays, making sure they have room between each scone.

7   Brush with milk and bake for approximately 18-20 minutes.

8   When fresh out of the oven sprinkle with parmesan, if you are using it. Sprigs of rosemary can be added as decoration.

Cook's Conversion Charts

Liquid, Volume, Herbs and Spices

Avoirdupois	Metric	Imperial
¼ tsp		1.2ml
½ tsp		2.5ml
1 tsp		5.0ml
½ tbsp (½ tsp)		7.5ml
1 tbsp (3 tsp)	½ fl oz	15ml
⅛ cup	1 fl oz	30ml
¼ cup (4 tbsp)	2 fl oz	60ml
⅓ cup (5 tbsp)	2 ½ fl oz	80ml
½ cup (8 tbsp)	4 fl oz	120ml
⅔ cup (10 tbsp)	5 fl oz	160ml
¾ cup (12 tbsp)	6 fl oz	180ml
1 cup (16 tbsp)	8 fl oz (½ pint)	250ml
1 ¼ cups	10 fl oz	300ml
1 ½ cups	12 fl oz	350ml
2 cups	16 fl oz (1 pint)	475ml
2 ½ cups	20 fl oz	625ml
3 cups	24 fl oz (1 ½ pints)	700ml
4 cups	32 fl oz (1 quart)	950ml
4 quarts	128 fl oz (1 gallon)	3.8l

Weight

Avoirdupois	Metric
¼ oz	7g
½ oz	15g
1 oz	30g
2 oz	55g
3 oz	85g
4 oz (¼ lb)	115g
5 oz (⅓ lb)	140g
6 oz	170g
7 oz	200g
8 oz (½ lb)	225g
9 oz	255g
10 oz (2/3 lb)	300g
11 oz	310g
12 oz (¾ lb)	340g
13 oz	370g
14 oz	400g
15 oz	425g
16 oz (1 lb)	450g
2 pounds	900g

Temperature

°F	°C
200	90
250	120
300	150
325	175
350	180
375	190
400	200
435	220
450	230
475	250
500	260

Baking Pan Sizes

	US	Volume	Metric	Volume
Rectangular	11 x 7 x inches	6 cups	28 x 18 x 5cm	1.4 litres
Rectangular	13 x 9 x 2 inches	4 cups	33 x 32 x 5cm	3.3 litres
Round	8 x 2 inches	6 cups	20 x 5cm	1.4 litres
Round	9 x 2 inches	8 cups	23 x 5cm	1.9 litres
Round	10 x 2 inches	1 cup	25 x 5cm	2.6 litres
Square	8 x 8 x 2 inches	8 cups	20 x 20 x 5cm	1.9 litres
Square	9 x 9 x 2 inches	10 cups	23 x 23 x 5cm	2.4 litres
Square	10 x 10 x 2 inches	12 cups	25 x 25 x 5cm	2.8 litres
Loaf	8 x 4 2 ½ inches	4 cups	20 x 10 x 6cm	948 ml
Loaf	9 x 5 x 3 inches	8 cups	23 x 13 x 8cm	1.9 litres

Please note
Conversions are not exact, they are rounded slightly for ease.